Dr. Kindergarten's Letter Sounds and Movement

Dr. Anika Harris Ed. D

Dr Kindergarten's Letter Sounds and Movement

Author

Dr. Anika Harris

Illustrator

Tommie S. Thornton

Kingdom Scribes Publishing, LLC.

Dr. Kindergarten's Letter Sounds and Movement

ISBN 978-0-578-11141-4

Dr. Anika N. Harris Ed. D
http://www.doctorkindergarten.com/

Kingdom Scribes Publishing, LLC.
www.kingdom-scribes.com
kingdomscribespublishing@yahoo.com

This book is dedicated to my parents,
Lawrence Harris and Jan Wyatt Harris.
Thank you for loving and believing in me.

These are a few of Dr. Kindergarten's students.
They and a few others are going to help Dr. Kindergarten with the alphabet!

You will say the chant, then the letter sound 3 times. Each time you say the letter sound you will make the movement that corresponds with the sound. Listed below are the directions for each movement.

A is for antlers –place a hand by each ear. Place thumbs by the top of each ear, spread fingers out and bend fingers down
B is for beating heart- use fist to touch chest near the heart
C is for cracking nuts- pretend to hold a nut and twist hands back and forth
D is for door knock- pretend to knock on a door with one fist
E is for echo- cup each hand and place hands around the mouth. Then say the sound
F is for funny fish- use both arms, bend elbows back and move the elbows in and out
G is for growing up- move hand up three times to show growth
H is for hard work- move right hand in a shoveling motion
I is for inch worm- move right hand up and down like a snake
J is for jumping- jump up and down
K is for kick ball- pretend to kick a ball
L is for looking- place one hand above the eyebrows then turn head to the right, left and then right
M is for milkshake- use one hand to make a circle on the stomach
N is for naptime- put hands together and place head on top on hands
O is for octopus-move both arms up and down like an octopus
P is for popcorn- bounce up and down
Q is for quiet please-place one finger on the lips
R is for raindrops- place both hands above the head and bring the hands down while moving fingers back and forth
S is for swimming- move arms in a swimming motion
T is for tiptoe- while standing in place tiptoe
U is for umbrella-put two fists on top of each other. Move the top fist upwards
V is for violin- pretend to hold a violin under the chin with one hand and play the violin with the other hand
W is for waxing- palms of both hands should move around in a circular motion
X is for x-ray- make an X with the arms and tap the arms together
Y is for yo-yo- pretend to throw a yo-yo in downward motion with one hand
Z is for zipper- pretend to zip up a jacket by placing one hand near the stomach and move upwards towards the chin

Aa

A

A is for Antlers

a - a - a

● ● ●

Bb

B

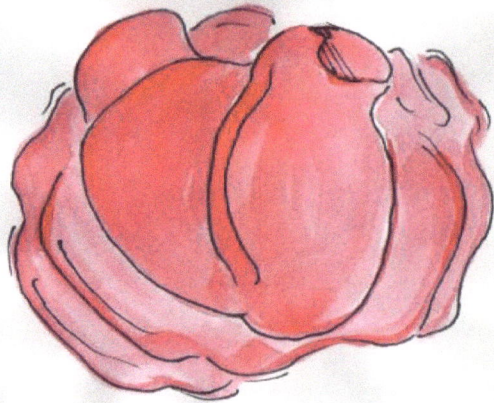

B is for Beating Heart

b - b - b

• • •

Cc

C

C is for Cracking Nuts

C - C - C

• • •

Dd

D

D is for Door Knock

D is for Door Knock
d - d - d
● ● ●

Ee

E

ECHO
ECHO
ECHO
ECHO

E is for Echo

e - e - e

• • •

Ff

F

F is for funny fish

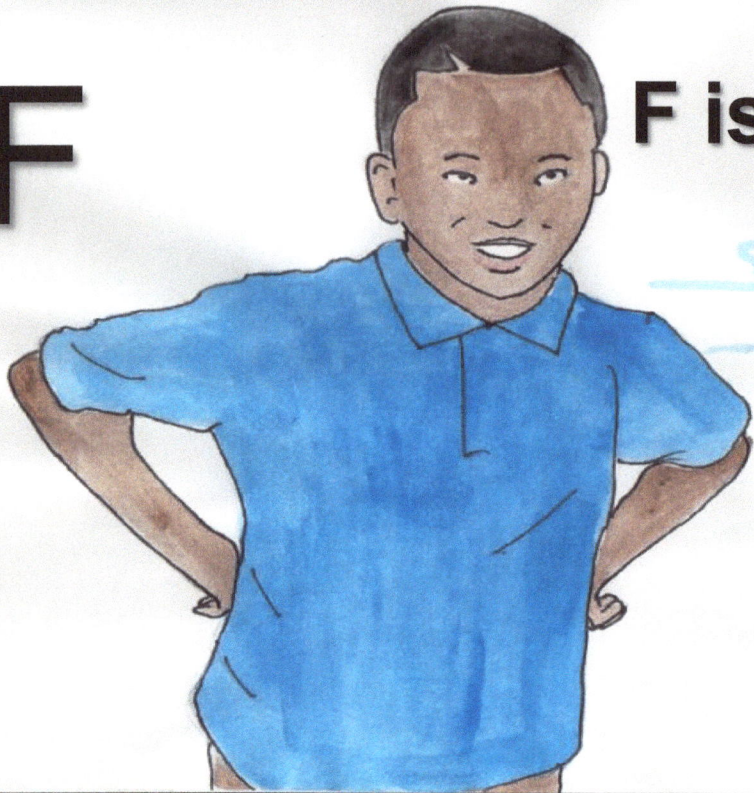

F is for
Funny Fish
f - f - f
● ● ●

Gg

G

G is for
Growing Up

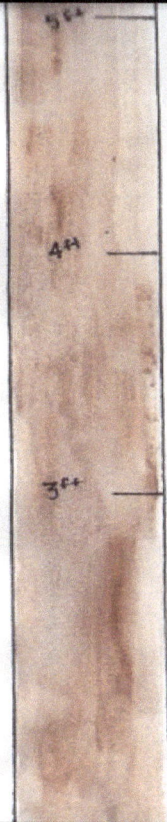

G is for Growing Up

g - g - g

●　　●　　●

Hh

H

H is for Hard Work

H is for Hard Work
h - h - h
● ● ●

Ii

I

I is for Inch Worm

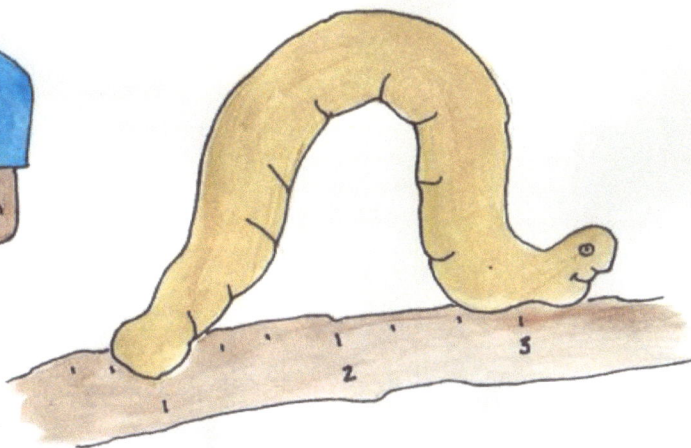

I is for Inch Worm

i - i - i

● ● ●

Jj

J

J is for Jumping

J is for Jumping
j - j - j
● ● ●

Kk

K

K is for Kick Ball

K is for Kick Ball

k - k - k

● ● ●

Ll

L is for
LOOKING

L is for Looking
l - l - l
● ● ●

Dr. Kindergarten's Letter Sounds and Movement

Mm

M

M is for Milk Shake

M is for Milk Shake

m - m - m
● ● ●

Nn

N

z z z

N is for Naptime

N is for
Naptime

n - n - n
• • •

Oo

O

O is for Octopus

O is for Octopus

o - o - o

Pp

P

POP!

P is for Popcorn

P is for Popcorn

p - p - p

● ● ●

Qq

Q

Q is for Quiet Please

Shhhh!

Q is for Quiet Please

q - q - q

Rr

R

R is for Rain Drops

R is for Rain Drops

r - r - r

● ● ●

Ss

S

S is for Swimming

S is for Swimming

s - s - s

● ● ●

Tt

T

T is for Tip Toe

T is for Tip Toe

t - t - t

● ● ●

Dr. Kindergarten's Letter Sounds and Movement

Uu

U

U is for Umbrella

U is for Umbrella

u - u - u

• • •

Vv

v

V is for Violin

V is for Violin

V - V - V

● ● ●

Ww

W

W is for Waxing

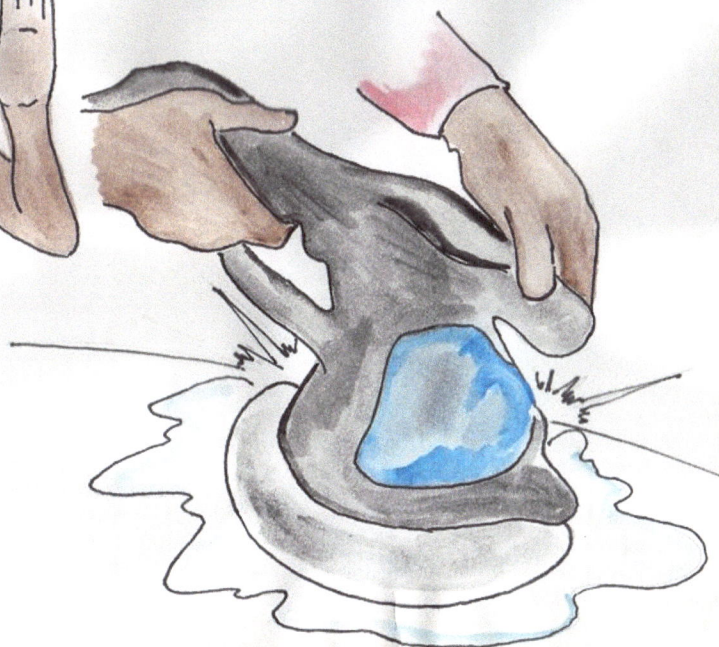

W is for Waxing

W - W - W

● ● ●

Xx

X

X is for X-Ray

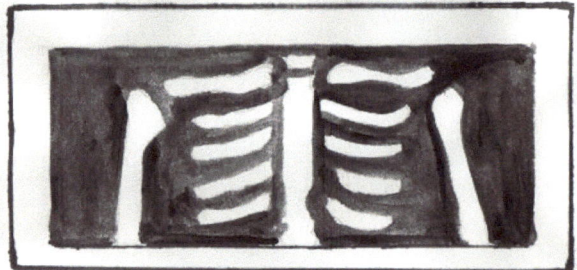

X is for X-Ray

X - X - X

● ● ●

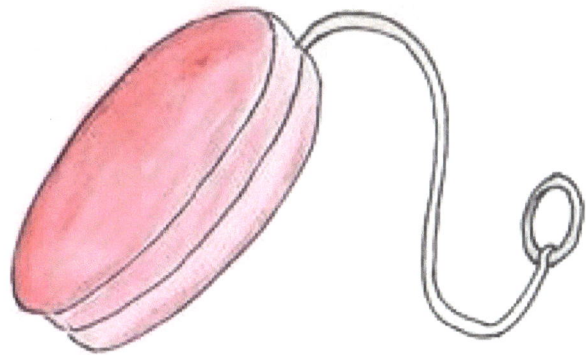

Y

Y is for Yo-Yo

Y is for Yo-Yo
y - y - y
● ● ●

Zz

Z

Z is for Zipper

Z is for Zipper

z - z - z

● ● ●

Dr. Anika Harris Ed. D
http://www.doctorkindergarten.com/

Kingdom Scribes Publishing, LLC
Now accepting manuscripts
www.kingdom-scribes.com

11.621   42740CB00002B/105 [209004540]